# SHOP
# SMART

PJ GRAY

# LIFESKILLS IN ACTION
## LIVING SKILLS

**MONEY**

Living on a Budget | Road Trip
Opening a Bank Account | The Guitar
Managing Credit | High Cost
Using Coupons | Get the Deal
Planning to Save | Something Big

**LIVING**

Smart Grocery Shopping | Shop Smart
Doing Household Chores | Keep It Clean
Finding a Place to Live | A Place of Our Own
Moving In | Pack Up
Cooking Your Own Meals | Dinner Is Served

**JOB**

Preparing a Résumé
Finding a Job
Job Interview Basics
How to Act Right on the Job
Employee Rights

**SADDLEBACK**
EDUCATIONAL PUBLISHING
www.sdlback.com

All source images from Shutterstock.com

ISBN-13: 978-1-68021-039-2
ISBN-10: 1-68021-039-4
eBook: 978-1-63078-345-7

Printed in Guangzhou, China
NOR/0116/CA21600020

20 19 18 17 16   1 2 3 4 5

One day Meg saw Jane after school. "Are you going to tell them?" Meg asked.

"Tell who about what?" Jane asked.

"Tell Dad and Pop. Tell them about Ray!"

Ray was Jane's new boyfriend. They had dated for a few months. Jane worked at the mall. That is where she met Ray.

Jane had not told her dads. She wanted to wait. She had to know it was love.

Jane met Ray after school. They kissed and held hands.

"I want to invite you to dinner," Jane said.

"Okay," Ray said. "Where do you want to go?"

Jane smiled. "No, silly. Dinner at my house. With my family."

"Oh," Ray said. He smiled back.

"Will you come to dinner?" she asked.

"Sure," Ray said. "I would like that."

Jane smiled. She was so happy.

"Wait!" Ray said.

"What's wrong?"

"You can cook?" Ray asked. Then he smiled.

Jane slapped his arm. "Very funny!"

Jane knew it was time to tell her dads. She waited until dinner that night.

"Can we talk?" Jane asked her dads.

Dad and Pop looked up from their food. "What's wrong?" Pop asked.

"Jane has a boyfriend!" Meg said.

"Meg!" Jane yelled. "Shut up!"

"Boyfriend?" Dad said. "Wow! When did this happen?"

"A few months ago," Jane said.

"Why didn't you tell us?" Pop asked.

"I waited until it was love."

"Is it love?" Dad asked.

"Yes, I think so," Jane said.

Dad and Pop smiled at Jane. "We want to meet him," Dad said.

"Invite him to Sunday dinner," Pop said.

Jane was happy. "I will cook!" she said.

Dad and Pop looked at each other. "Okay. Give me your shopping list," Dad said.

"Yes," Pop said. "We will shop for you."

"No," Jane said. "I will take care of it all."

"Are you sure?" Dad and Pop said.

Meg began to laugh.

"Very funny," Jane said with a smile. "Yes, I am sure."

Jane thought about the meal. She would roast a turkey. She would make stuffing. Ray liked stuffing. Her dads liked it too. And she wanted to bake a cake for dessert.

It was Friday. Jane saw Meg during a break at school.

"Are you ready for Sunday?" Meg asked.

"I think so," Jane said.

"When will you grocery shop?" Meg asked. "You have a lot to buy."

Jane had to work the next day. She would have to grocery shop after work. She needed to cook on Sunday.

"Don't you work tomorrow?" Meg asked Jane.

"I can shop tomorrow night after work."

"Won't you be too tired?" Meg asked.

"Yeah," Jane said. "I should do most of it tonight."

Jane's cell phone rang. She looked at the text.

"Who is it?" Meg asked.

"It's Ray. He wants to go out tonight."

"Tonight?" Meg asked. "But you have to grocery shop."

"I know," Jane said.

"What are you going to do?"

"I want to see Ray," Jane said.

Meg gave Jane a look.

"Don't look at me like that," Jane said. "It will be fine. I still have time to shop."

Jane sent a text back to Ray. She did not grocery shop that night.

Saturday came. Jane worked all day. She was very tired. And she was hungry. But she had to go to the market.

Jane had not made a list. She took a shopping cart. Then she went through the store. Up and down aisles.

She saw a candy bar. It looked good. And she was hungry. She put it in her cart.

Jane tried to think about the Sunday dinner. "What did I want to make? Oh yes, a turkey."

Jane looked around the store. A sign in the back said Meat. She went there and found turkeys. Some were big. Others were small. Jane did not know which one to get.

A man came by. He had a name tag. It said "John" and "Meat Dept. Manager."

"May I help you?" he asked.

"Yes," said Jane. "I am going to roast a turkey tomorrow. We have five people. Which one should I get?"

"Look for an 8-pound turkey," the man said. He showed her some.

Jane found a turkey. She kept shopping. But it was hard to think of what she needed.

Jane sent a text to Meg. "At the store," the text read. "Very tired. Need help. Call me back."

Meg did not call back.

Jane thought about the meal. "Stuffing," she said. "I need stuffing."

She checked each aisle. Finally, she found the stuffing. There were many kinds.

Jane looked at the boxes. She picked one. It had a picture of stuffing on it. And it looked right.

Jane got eggs and milk. Then she went to the checkout lane.

"Paper or plastic," a girl asked.

"Um, plastic, I guess," said Jane.

Jane came home and unpacked the bags. It was very late.

She looked inside a bag. It had the eggs in it. But Jane had set the turkey on top of that bag. The eggs had been crushed. They were broken. It was a mess.

Jane was mad. But she cleaned up the mess. Then she unpacked the bags and went to bed.

Sunday came. Jane was scared. She had so much to do. And she had little time to do it.

Jane put the turkey in the oven. She looked at the kitchen clock.

Next she got out the stuffing. But she needed some things. She had not bought them last night.

"I will bake the cake now," she said.

Jane read her cookbook. She did not have vegetable oil. And she forgot. She had no eggs. They were crushed!

Jane looked at the wall clock again. She also looked at her watch.

"Meg!" Jane called to her sister. "Help!"

Meg ran into the kitchen.

"I need your help!" said Jane. "We have to go to the market."

"Didn't you go yesterday?" Meg asked.

"I forgot some things," Jane said. "Didn't you get my text?"

"No," Meg replied. "Didn't you make a list?"

"No!" Jane said. "But now I will. We have to hurry!"

Jane and Meg read the cookbook.

"Make a list!" Meg cried out.

They made a grocery list. Jane checked the oven. The turkey was cooking.

"Let's go now," Meg said. "We'll get back before it's done."

They raced to the market. They grabbed two carts.

Jane held up her grocery list. "Here, Meg," Jane said.

Jane tore the list in two. She gave Meg half. "We can shop twice as fast! Let's do this!"

Jane and Meg used their lists. They found all of their items. They raced back to the line to pay.

Jane looked at the bagger. "Could you give me the bag with the eggs?" she asked. "I want to keep them on top."

Meg smiled at Jane. Jane and Meg raced home.

They took the turkey from the oven. It smelled so good.

Meg looked at her watch. "Ray is coming soon," she said.

"I won't finish in time!" Jane said. "I wanted this to be perfect."

Meg held out her hand. "I can help," Meg said. "Don't worry."

Dad and Pop came into the kitchen. "We can help too," Pop said.

"Yes," Dad agreed. "Don't worry. We will all help."

Jane hugged each of them. Then she smiled. "Let's do this!"

What mistakes did Jane make during her first trip to the grocery store? Want to learn more about how being a smart shopper can save you time and money?

JUST *flip* THE BOOK!

# LIFESKILLS IN ACTION

# Smart Grocery Shopping

JANE GARDNER

# LIFESKILLS IN ACTION

## LIVING SKILLS

**MONEY**

Living on a Budget | Road Trip
Opening a Bank Account | The Guitar
Managing Credit | High Cost
Using Coupons | Get the Deal
Planning to Save | Something Big

**LIVING**

Smart Grocery Shopping | Shop Smart
Doing Household Chores | Keep It Clean
Finding a Place to Live | A Place of Our Own
Moving In | Pack Up
Cooking Your Own Meals | Dinner Is Served

**JOB**

Preparing a Résumé
Finding a Job
Job Interview Basics
How to Act Right on the Job
Employee Rights

SADDLEBACK
EDUCATIONAL PUBLISHING
www.sdlback.com

All source images from Shutterstock.com

ISBN-13: 978-1-68021-039-2
ISBN-10: 1-68021-039-4
eBook: 978-1-63078-345-7

3 4873 00522 4365

Printed in Guangzhou, China
NOR/0116/CA21600020

20 19 18 17 16   1 2 3 4 5

We all need to eat.

It can seem easy growing up.

Someone makes us **food**.

School lunches.

Meals at home.

Eating out.

But what about when we are on our own?

Fast food is easy to get.

It may cost only a few dollars.

But it is not healthy.

The food is high in fat.

And sugar.

Making your own meals is better.

But that means buying food.

**Groceries**.

This takes time.

There are many choices to make.

The key is to shop smart.

How? Make a plan.

Buy food for the week.

Start with a **shopping list**.

Write down the things you need.

First check the kitchen.

See what is there.

Look in the cupboards.

Open the refrigerator.

And the freezer.

Out of milk?

Low on cereal?

Add those items to the list.

What about **coupons**?

They can save you money.

Put them by your list.

Here's a tip.

Do not shop if you are hungry.

Hunger makes people buy more food.

They tend to make unhealthy choices.

Candy bars. Chips. Soda.

These are **impulse buys**.

They cost extra money.

And they are not good for you.

Shop smart.

Have a snack before going to the store.

Then you won't be hungry.

Most stores have a printed ad.

Pick one up at the front.

Check it to see what's on sale.

Are any items on your list?

Mark those.

Most grocery stores are big.

They have many **departments**.

There are **aisles** and shelves.

It can seem confusing.


But stores are set up to help.

Signs tell where things are.

Each department has a sign.

Every aisle has one too.

Use the signs as guides.

It makes shopping faster.

Learn which foods are in each department.

Look for the signs that say **dairy**.

Eggs, milk, and cheese will be there.

There will be a meat department.

This has chicken, beef, and fish.

The **produce** department has fruits.

And vegetables.

Most stores are set up the same.

It makes it easier to find things.

Cans and boxes are in the middle.

Frozen foods are there too.

Fresh items are in the back, along the walls.

They are in refrigerators.

Fruits and vegetables may be near the front.

Each department has a **manager**.

They are there to help.

A recipe may call for one kind of lettuce.

It is hard to find.

The produce manager can help.

A store may have an item on sale.

But it may run out of that item.

A manager can give out a **rain check**.

This is a written note. It is a promise.

Use it to buy the item next time.

You will get the sale price.

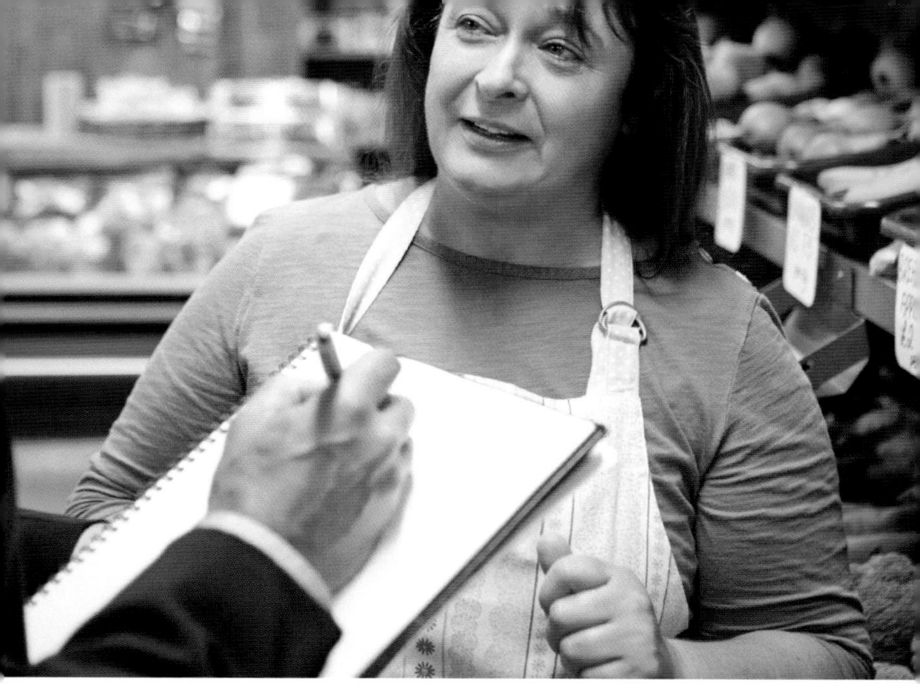

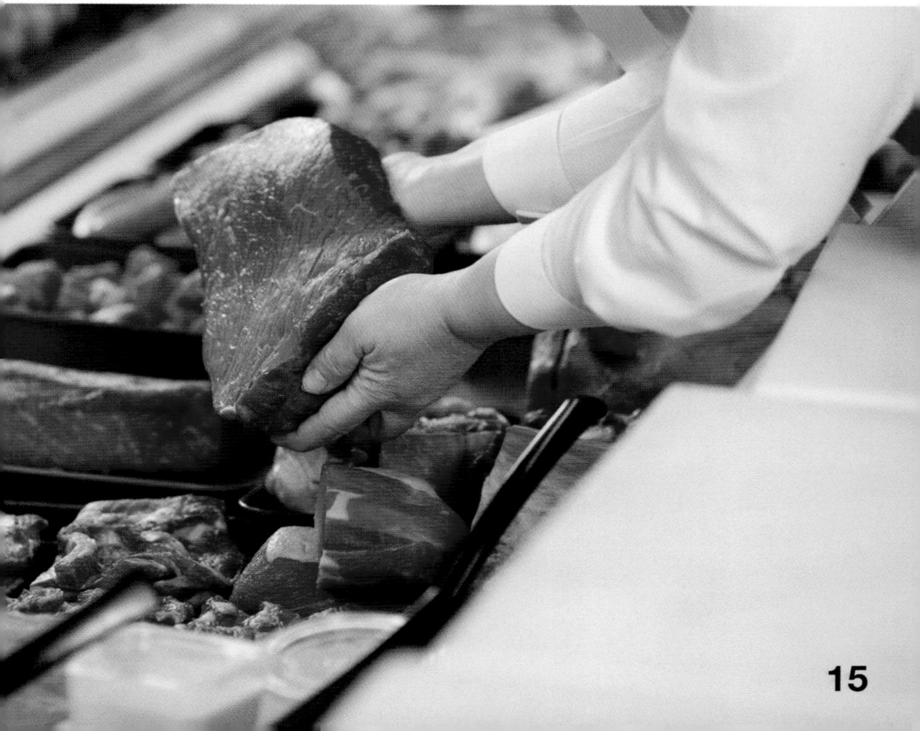

**Prices**.

They tell what things cost.

Saving money is easy.

How? Compare prices.

Buy things that cost less.

Think about bread.

There are many kinds. Each one has a price.

Compare them and then choose.

**Name brands** can cost a lot.

**Store brands** cost less.

Think about it.

Is the cheaper one just as good?

Try it and see.

That's shopping smart.

Think about **amounts** too.

This means the number of things to buy.

Will one loaf of bread be enough?

If not, get two.

Buy the amount needed for a week.

Foods can come in more than one **size**.

Tomato sauce is like that.

There are big cans and small cans.

Choose the size you need.

Make healthy choices.

Look at **nutrition labels**.

They are printed on packages.


Read the ingredients.

Vitamins. Sugar and salt. Fat content.

Know what's in the food.

Be aware of how much is there.

Shopping healthy is smart.

# Nutrition Facts

**Serving Size 5 oz. (144g)**
**Servings Per Container 4**

**Amount Per Serving**

**Calories** 310          **Calories** from Fat  100

| | % Daily Value* |
|---|---|
| **Total Fat** 15g | **21%** |
| Saturated Fat 2.6g | **17%** |
| Trans Fat 1g | |
| **Cholesterol** 118mg | **39%** |
| **Sodium** 560mg | **28%** |
| **Total Carbohydrate** 12g | **4%** |
| Dietary Fiber 1g | **4%** |
| Sugars 1g | |
| **Protein** 24g | |

| | | | |
|---|---|---|---|
| **Vitamin A** 1% | • | **Vitamin C** 2% | |
| **Calcium** 2% | • | **Iron** 5% | |

*Percent Daily Values are based on a 2,000 calorie diet. Your daily values may be higher or lower depending on your calorie needs:

| | Calories | 2,000 | 2,500 |
|---|---|---|---|
| Total Fat | Less Than | 65g | 80g |
| Saturated Fat | Less Than | 20g | 25g |
| Cholesterol | Less Than | 300mg | 300mg |
| Sodium | Less Than | 2,400mg | 2,400mg |
| Total Carbohydrate | | 300g | 375g |
| Dietary Fiber | | 25g | 30g |

Calories per gram:
    Fat 9  •  Carbohydrate 4  •  Protein 4

**Expiration dates** are important.

Most foods have one.

Find the words "Use by" or "Sell by."

There will be a date.

Keep that in mind.

Expired food can make people sick.

SELL BY OCT 14 08:53

Other items have expiration dates too.

Vitamins. Toothpaste. Dog food.

Always check the date.

Foods in cans and boxes last longer.

Other foods go bad fast.

Milk. Cheese. Meats.

These are **perishables**.

These foods should be kept in the refrigerator.

Always look at the expiration date.

Buy only what is needed for the week.

Look at boxes. Check for **damage**.

They may be open or torn.

Pick another one.

Check the food too.

Open egg cartons. Are any eggs cracked?

If so, get a new carton.

Some damaged foods are **marked down**.

They have a lower price.

Foods about to expire may be marked down too.

They may be in a basket near the front or back of the store.

Look for a sign that says "special" or "sale."

The boxes or cans may not look good.

But the food is safe.

Just be sure to check the date.

It may be soon.

Use the food before that time.

There are other ways to save.

Look for weekly **specials**.

"Ten boxes of crackers for $10.00."

It seems like a deal.

But it may not be.

That is a lot of crackers.

Ask a store worker.

You may be able to buy one.

And still get the sale price.

Store ads won't say that.

Check to be sure.

Grocery stores are **convenient**.

They have many services.

People can get a lot done in one place.

Rent movies.

Pay bills.

Buy flowers.

Many stores have a bank.

Doing everything in one place saves time.

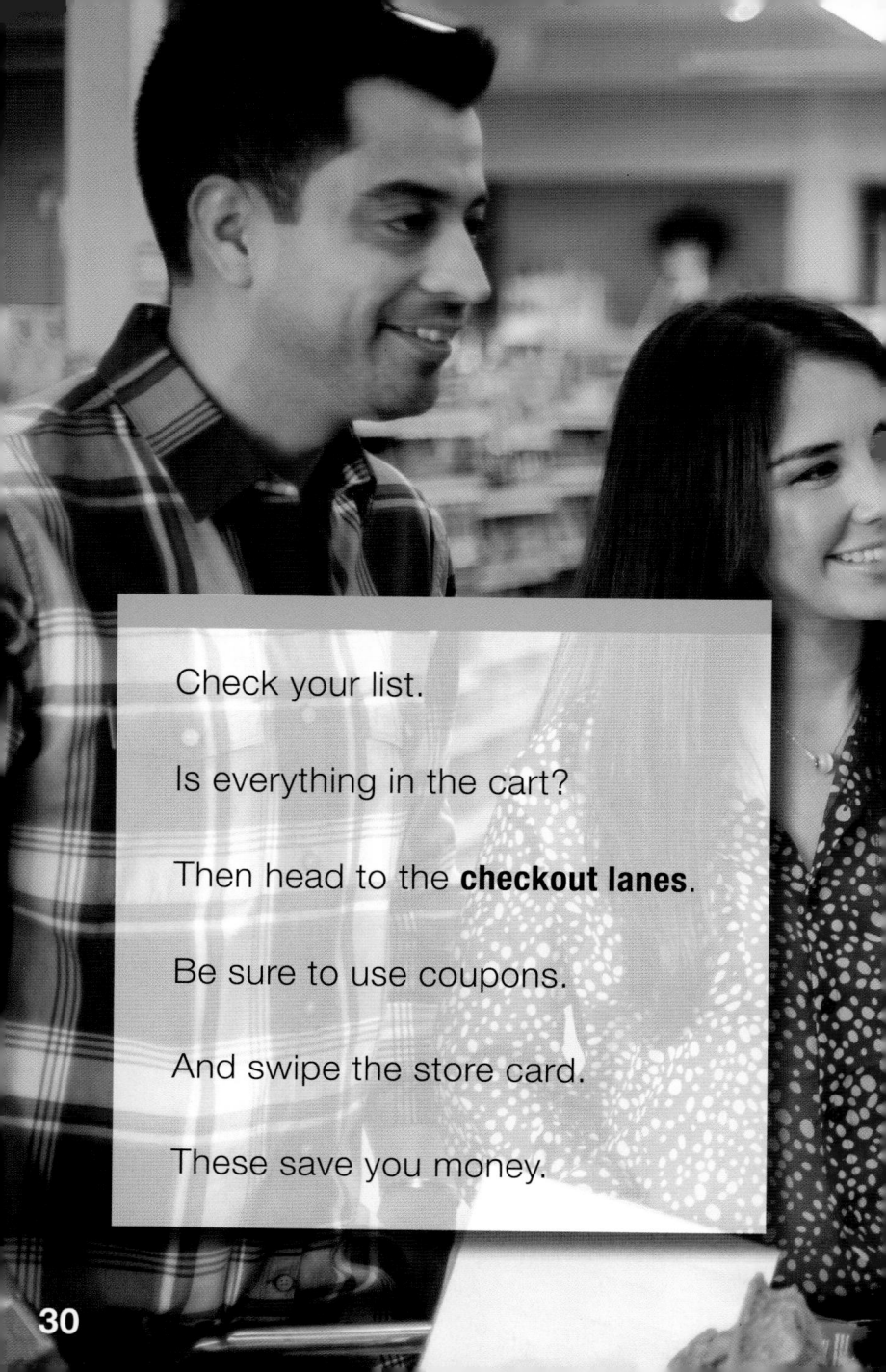

Check your list.

Is everything in the cart?

Then head to the **checkout lanes**.

Be sure to use coupons.

And swipe the store card.

These save you money.

Grocery shopping takes time.

There is a lot to think about.

Make good choices.

Choose healthy foods.

Check prices.

It's worth it.

You will save money.

And eat well.

**That's shopping smart!**

JUST *Flip* THE BOOK!

SHOP
SMART
PJ GRAY

What happens when a person
goes to the grocery store
without a list? That is what Jane
finds out in *Shop Smart.* Want to
read on?